The 21 Day Budgeting Challenge

Learn How to Set up a Budget, Pay off Debts and Make the Most of Your Money

by
Olivia S. Taylor

Contents

Introduction

Maybe you're thinking that the only thing worse than budgeting is reading a book about budgeting. And you may be right. But with this book, my hope is that I can change your mind. My hope is that at the end of this short guide, you will feel more in control of your spending habits, have clearer and more meaningful financial goals and, most importantly, have a little fun while doing it.

For some strange reason, learning about personal finance and how to take control of money is something we neglect to teach children at school. Perhaps we can blame our culture for laying a shroud of fear and secrecy over a simple fact of life that nobody can avoid: we all need to handle money. And yet if you ask the average person to list their top three life worries right now, you can guarantee most of them will mention dismal finances.

If you're sick of feeling broke, of having lots of things but nothing that you actually love, of working hard but not feeling as though you're working for anything, then read on. Money is a force of nature, and with the right mindset, it can become a tool to help you reach your goals, embrace who you are and get the most out of life.

In this book, we'll look at ways to uncover your own personal psychology behind money, as well as practical methods to make and reach finance goals. From saving pennies here and there by cutting out mindless spending to rethinking your approach to saving entirely, we'll tackle your money issues the simple way: day by day. We'll consider realistic ways to save money, but also look in depth at what it really means to live a minimalist life and what the true value of the items in our lives actually is.

After reading through this simple 21 day budgeting challenge, my goal is that the shroud of mystery hanging over money is lifted a little, and you feel inspired to engage with it in a new, more meaningful way. So let's get started!

Day 1

Your Money Personality

U gh. Budgets. Next to going on a diet or doing your taxes, budgeting has to be one of the most tedious and unpleasant things. It may be weird to start a budgeting challenge book this way, but the first thing we're going to do is unpack our beliefs and ideas around the idea of budgeting.

So... what's your money personality?

Maybe you're a **"money martyr"** - you'd secretly rather live in luxury but you believe that money is more or less the root of evil and you're going to punish yourself by buying off-brand cereal and staying in on Saturdays. You feel so fabulous being so pious, but you fall off the wagon regularly and buy yourself something expensive and ridiculous when the deprivation just becomes too much.

Maybe you're a **"hippie"** - you believe, like, if you just open yourself up and become receptive to the abundance of the universe, then life will deliver, you know? It's all well and good but you spend the first chunk of your salary on imported Sandalwood temple oil and then blame Capitalism when you have to eat rice and tuna for three days while you wait to get paid again.

Maybe you're a **"big spender"** - you're a generous person, and the best way to show people you love them is to treat them to a steak dinner and drinks - hey, don't worry, the bill's on you! A big spender likes to take care of people, to boast a little, to eat, drink and be merry. The other part of this money personality is abject depression at the thought of opening your credit card statements.

Maybe you're an **"ostrich"** - if you don't talk about money problems, then they can't hurt you, right? You keep your head in the sand and pray it all blows over. Maybe you had parents who were bad with money, maybe you grew up poor or maybe you've learnt to think of money as something big, scary and complicated - so you don't actually know how much you make each month, your online banking password or how to buy stocks.

Maybe you're a **"scrooge"** - money is a competition, and whatever happens, you refuse to lose. You won't be left with nothing. You'll be the squirrel that hoards every last acorn and plan to have the last laugh when winter comes. Money isn't for using, it's for having, and you plan to have a whole bunch, one saved penny at a time. Trouble is, you're a big old pain in the ass about it.

Of course, I'm mostly not being serious about these money types, but I am serious about this: people have relationships with money just the same as they do to everything and everyone else. Get to the root of your relationship with money and you start to get an idea of how you can restructure your attitudes and habits.

Today's task: try to identify your "money personality". Do you have any strengths? Any blind spots?

Day 2

Commit to Your Motivation

I'll keep this short: to achieve any goal, you need to, well... have one in the first place. If you journal, now would be the perfect time to make a note of what exactly you're trying to accomplish. It may be as simple as "save $100 more each month" or it may be as ambitious as "completely change my financial lifestyle."

Whatever it is, the first step is to put it down. Do whatever you need to to assure yourself that it's really happening. Write out a "contract", tell others about your plan or give yourself a deadline where you'll appraise your progress.

Once you know the what (and the *why*), you can focus more clearly on the how.

Day 3

Life's Little Vices

Let's jump right in. A friend of mine wanted to save money and she thought an easy target would be to cut down on how much money she blew at Starbucks everyday. Starbucks is overpriced, right? Coffee is just a luxury, right? So, it should be no big deal to cut back and save a bit extra each month. Just think of what she could with the extra $100 she spends on fancy coffee every month.

The trouble is, by the time day four rolled around, it had become clear to my friend and everyone around her exactly how valuable that few dollars spent at Starbucks each day really was. While it's true that it was a "luxury", that she could get cheaper coffee elsewhere etc., the fact is that in reality, that daily cup of fancy coffee was a sanity-saving ritual for her. It was how she started each day, it was armor for whatever tribulations lay ahead, it literally revved her up, kept her alert and gave her a bit of pleasure and enjoyment in what was otherwise a stressful day. Kind of a bargain, when you think about it.

It may seem like an easy question - how much a thing costs you - but think it through. I'm the last person to suggest that frittering money away on overpriced coffee is a good idea, but at the same time ... it *might* be.

Today's the day to have a closer look at all these little vices. For my friend, it was an obscenely large Starbucks coffee. For you it may be smoking or throwing away money on alcohol on the weekends, or online shoe shopping or impulse gadget and game buys or expensive Chinese take out from the place down the road which is really just serving you rice and mystery meat.

You could be all saintly about these little vices and just say no, but you and I both know how hard this is. Why? Because those bad habits are there for a reason. As long as a little spending habit is fulfilling some need, you're going to keep right on doing it.

The trick, then, if you want to cut it out and do something less expensive, is to find out what that need is. This way, you can consciously choose to find ways to satisfy it that are cheaper. Maybe healthier, too. So have a good look. Be honest and add up how much you're really paying to have your little vices each month. You may feel like high end manicures every two weeks are essential, but if you see how much they're costing you, you may think again.

Your bad habits may be there because they act as: distraction from something unpleasant, boredom with life in general, soothing from stress and sadness, an easy "solution' when you're too lazy to do better or a habit from sheer momentum. A bad habit can be part of your identity, a way to socialize or something your family or culture promotes.

Once you've identified the need, find a cheaper way to fulfill it. If getting expensive manicures fulfills your need to be cared for and acts as a way to de-stress and give yourself a confidence boost, see if you can scale them back and do things that give you that same feeling for free: meditation, seeking advice from friends, sleeping and eating well or, gasp!, doing your own nails.

Today's task: root out those little vices and replace them with, well, "budget vices". If you're like my friend who becomes intolerable without her vice, you have my permission to indulge.

Day 4

The Slow Death of Debt and How to Get Out

I'm sure I don't have to tell you that debt is bad. I'm sure I don't have to explain to you the crushing psychological effects - after all, we've all experienced it. Some unfinished business hangs over your head, subtly tainting everything you do. You are never truly free when you owe somebody. You're on borrowed money, borrowed time, and borrowed peace of mind.

Practically, debt doesn't make much sense either. For the privilege of stressing over what you owe, you pay a premium in the form of interest. If you're lucky, this interest can be so steep that you may pay debt down each month just to stay in exactly the same place.

Health, happiness and all those good things in life can't really exist if you don't have a sense that you are free to act, free to work hard and enjoy the results. The quickest way to kill your motivation is to work hard so that you can pay back money you've already spent. Instead of being able to look to the future and make plans, you're looking to the past, trying to play catch up.

Grim, right?

Nevertheless debt is a real, scary problem for a lot of people. There isn't enough room in this book to discuss sound ways out of a debt hole if that's where you happen to be. But do take some time right now to understand the difference between good debt and bad debt. If you take on debt that will add value to your life and make it easier for you to earn more later on, it's good debt. Taking on debt for things that degrade faster than you can pay them off is not smart.

Killing debt is first and foremost a psychological problem. You need to take a look at the reality of your situation, no matter how ugly it is. Identify those debts that carry the highest interest and make a plan to tackle them first. Look at your budget (more on this later) and decide how much you can devote each month to wiping out your debt.

Sell things, cut back on expenses, do what you need to: debt is much easier to deal with if you have a plan to stick to. Pay more than the minimum each month on credit cards and see if you can consolidate loans. Here, chatting with a financial planner can be the single best move if you're serious about becoming debt free.

Today's goal: if your debt is substantial and messing with your peace of mind, get on the phone now to book an appointment with your bank's financial advisor. Debt is a common problem - don't be ashamed or nervous about asking for help. In an hour you can decide on your plan of action. Even if your debt is small, see what you can do to reduce or eliminate it.

Day 5

Do You Over-Consume?

Being a rampant over-consumer is like being a bad driver: somebody has to be doing it and yet nobody ever admits it might be them. Maybe you think that you're not guilty of over-consumption because you're not "wealthy", you don't buy designer brands and you always clear your plate.

But materialism as a lifestyle is far more subtle than this. Here are some clues that much of your spending is not, in fact, core to your happiness in life:

- When there's a celebration, new event, holiday or trip, your first thought is "I have to buy stuff". For many people, birthday celebrations, Christmas, Sunday afternoons or family visits simply can't happen unless they buy and consume something.

- You have at one point or other bought something because you thought it would, directly or indirectly, make you happy. Then, it didn't do that, and you bought something else for the same reason. In a consumerist society, you see, the problem is never solved. You are always dissatisfied, so you keep buying.

- Your home is filled with items you loved at first but immediately lost interest in the moment you brought them home.

- You feel like a big part of your identity is tied into the things you own, and worry that without them, you won't be yourself. What's a snazzy young businessman without his vehicle? What's a free-spirited artist without her flowing skirts and bangles?

- You feel numb. You imagined a certain thing would give you pleasure but after you own that thing, suddenly the bar shifts and you need another, better thing to give you pleasure. Until you have tons of things ...and suspiciously little pleasure.

Really looking closely at your relationship to material things and money can be an eye-opening experience. It's difficult to take a moment and step out of the materialistic cage we all grow up in and live our lives in. Constant, pervasive advertising and media convince us on all sides that buying things is a way of life, a way to solve problems, an identity, a source of love and meaning, basically, everything.

But the fact is that they are just things. Some objects may be useful tools to acquire certain psychological states, but they are not the same thing as those psychological states. A fast internet connection, a nice new laptop and a computer game can all lead to fun and enjoyment, sure, but in the end they are just things. Fun and enjoyment is what's important to you, and already available to you right now, without having to buy anything. Really.

Today's exercise is to meditate on some of the "stuff" in your life. Take a good look at it and see if it's really serving you, or whether it's just eating money and taking up space. Challenge your own assumptions. Do you need it? Does it make you happy? What would happen if it wasn't there?

Day 6

Minimalism vs. Materialism

Minimalism is one of my favorite things. Minimalism is like a nice, clean knife, cutting away at the junk of life and leaving behind a neat, tidy idea. But the joy of minimalism is that it's something you do, and not only something you read about. If you're curious, you can have a look at the 21-Day Minimalism Challenge on Amazon.

Minimalism, contrary to what our capitalist and consumerist world would have us believe, is not about doing without, or suffering, or deprivation and being unhappy. It's about elegance. It's about enough.

Many people recoil in horror at the idea of enough, feeling that it's more or less the same as not enough, which is strange when you think about it. Having enough means your needs are filled, without waste. You don't spend time or money or effort on things that don't serve you past that need. You have your values and goals in life, and items are merely tools: if they add to the effort, you keep them; if they don't, there's no room in your life for them.

Yesterday, I asked you to look at the objects in your life and assess them in terms of how good they were at fulfilling your happiness. But you can have other goals, too. What satisfies one may not satisfy another. When you start with the goal, though, you can then choose the objects accordingly. You control the items in your life, rather than them controlling you.

Today's exercise: Look at some of your largest and most serious possessions and ask yourself, do they serve your highest values and goals? House, car, electronics, wardrobe, anything really. If they aren't serving you, why the hell do you have them?

Day 7

Finding Your Priorities

I'm sure you know the feeling. You get home, take a peek in your wallet and briefly wonder, "damn, didn't I have more money in here?"

This, friends, is mindless spending, and its danger lies in the fact that you don't even notice you're doing it. Somebody might glibly tell you, "oh, we don't spend that much on take-out" but take a closer look and everyone would be horrified at how much they're spending without realizing it.

It seems simple, but many people fail with budgeting because they are solving a problem they think they have but don't, all the while ignoring a problem they do have but think they don't. Call it a financial blind spot. The only way to make realistic changes to your spending is to get an accurate "before" picture. How much are you really spending now, and on what?

Today's challenge is to do a quick financial diagnostic and see where your money is really going. I'm not going to ask you to start today (because then you'll just cheat!) but to look backwards at what you've already spent this last week.

Be meticulous. Every coffee, every coin that went into a SPCA tin, every coupon and every second round of beers you bought. Go back in time and note everything you've spent in the 7 day period preceding now. Look at bank statements/notifications to help you. Two things may happen:

Thing one - you may discover it's really hard. This is a big clue that the challenge for you will be to become more mindful of your spending.

Thing two - you may start to notice some shocking trends. While you imagine buying a small chocolate or candy every day after lunch is just "a few bucks" here and there, it may be quite a surprise to see that it adds up to a whopping $50 in the course of a month.

You'll know that your spending in one area needs to be managed if you have this panicked, visceral reaction. Could you do something more interesting and more valuable with an extra $50 each week, something a little more enriching and enjoyable than the occasional candy after lunch?

It's much easier to formulate a budget when you don't think of merely reducing your expenditure, but of redistributing it. It's sad and boring to think of what you can do without, but infinitely more exciting to imagine if you could take the money you already spend and spend it on something you care much more about. This is the best kind of "saving" - spending the same amount of money and getting more happiness and meaning out of it at the end of the day.

Today, see if you can identify 3 areas where you're overspending, and 3 other areas where you're under-spending. Later, you can draw up a budget that changes up these priorities so you can maximize on the things that are actually going to make you happy.

Day 8

Down to the Wire

O *k, let's start budgeting.*

You've had a little think about your own values, your own spending habits and your own little vices that may or may not be sapping cash out of your life. Now, it's time to draw up a budget that respects your unique situation.

Here, it pays to think of a budget not as some holy decree sent from down a mountain top, but a guide, one that can be changed in time depending on what's happening in your life. A budget should be a little curious, kind of like a question asking, does this make me happier? What about this?

Step one: identify the non-negotiables. There are actually not as many as you think. Unless you're planning to make big life changes soon, this means your rent, council tax, utilities, more or less a fixed amount for monthly care and gas payments ... that kind of thing.

Step two: identify the sort-of-negotiables. This category includes things like food, since you can save here and spend less, but unless you plan on becoming a breatharian, you can't reduce this down to nothing. Include other things with wiggle room, like private health insurance if you get it, toiletries and medicines, clothing, daycare, TV, data, phone and internet costs and the like. Include savings and debt repayments here, too.

Step three: identify waste. These are things you don't need, not even a little bit, and need to cut out completely. This includes your bad impulse makeup buying, gambling money you really could use more wisely or fees and charges you actually don't need to be paying.

Step four: make small changes. Not big ones. Draw up a spreadsheet where you allocate what you need to spend on the non-negotiables and cut out the waste. What you have left can go to the sort-of-negotiables.

Tweak things a little, giving more money to those three things you identified as being important and taking away money from the 3 less important things. Those items that can be manipulated a little (such as food) can be reduced by about 10% without you noticing. Promise.

Eventually, you should have a budget that does a few things:

1. Successfully makes provision for the things each month you have to pay for, no matter what,

2. Gives you a little motivation to save money on those things you're maybe spending too much on,

3. Makes no allowance for bad habits and wasteful spending,

4. Has room for savings (try a minimum of 5%, but 10% is better) and debt repayments (should be more than the minimum) and,

5. Is not hellishly unpleasant. Since you're not a robot, you won't like staying on a money diet that restricts all the good things in life completely. Have room for those things that make you happy, keep you healthy and relaxed and add meaning to your life. Otherwise what's the point of any of it?

Take a good hard look at what you've created, and be willing to let it all go. You may try it for a week and find it's not realistic. Don't abandon the whole endeavor, come back to the drawing board and hash out a plan that will work. Rinse and repeat.

Day 9

It's All About the Cash Money

Especially for those loosey-goosey, go with the flow types, this sort of structure can feel a bit stifling. For some people, merely having some "rules" means they immediately start to itch to break them. But a set budget is actually a freedom. It's actually a relief. Spend a bit of time upfront with a budget and you save yourself stress and worry for the rest of the time. Know that as long as you stick to the budget, you can reach your goals.

Today, you're going to put your new budget into action.

And you're going to do it with cash. A few caveats: you may eventually decide that going all-cash doesn't work for your lifestyle. That's fine. But this is a good exercise to do anyway. Why? Because cash grounds you. Cash is something you can see (and you can also see it flying out of your wallet). Cash isn't some abstract idea of money somewhere in a bank or on a computer screen. It's real.

At the start of this new week, draw cash from an ATM to last you for the week ahead, according to your budget. Then, put away all your bankcards - you won't touch them again until a week has passed.

It may help to put different cash amounts into envelopes devoted to different areas of spending, but whatever you do, understand that if you spend this money, it's gone. No credit. If you dip into one category to spend on another, you simply have less money all round. Relax and know that you've sorted out your priorities, now it's just a question of actually doing it. Make a note of how you feel when you first try this. Panicked? Relieved?

Day 10

Stop Being a Drug Addict

Yes, I know you're not a drug addict. But in a way …you kind of are.

If you've ever made an impulse buy, been swayed by an urgent sale or got a rush of happiness after buying a long-coveted goodie, then yes, you're as much under the influence of drugs as anyone has ever been. The drug in this case is dopamine, and spending can release as much of it as falling in love or smoking crack.

Ok, maybe not quite as bad as that but you catch my drift.

In this little analogy, massive chain stores, advertisers and credit card companies are all drug-pushers. They want you to feel that dopamine rush so you'll keep handing them money. Many brands' entire sales mechanism rests on the power of invoking this pleasurable response in the brain. We're tricked by sales, ads, sneaky techniques and much more into thinking that buying is a pleasurable, indispensable act.

It isn't, of course. Here are some ways to lessen the impact of things designed to keep you coughing up. The good news is that once you sober up and get used to looking at things carefully, it becomes easier and easier.

- If you see something you like, sleep on it before you buy. If you still want it 2 days later, it's less likely to be an impulse purchase.

- Keep receipts and tags so you can return things once the shine wears off.

- If it's a question of a big sale - ask yourself whether you'd buy an item even if it wasn't on sale. If the answer is no, watch out, you may be the victim of persuasive sales.

- Try to imagine a new purchase in your actual life, as it is now. Don't fantasize about the role a new thing will play in your ideal, one-day-perfect life. This is an illusion. You are not a mannequin or an airbrushed model in a magazine. How is that pair of shoes or kitchen appliance really going to feature in your life?

- Don't go shopping hungry, bored or stressed. *Ever*.

- Read online reviews and research new purchases well to make sure you're getting a good deal. Buying online also lessens the chance you buy things because of environmental influences in the store.

- Be firm with salespeople and don't let them bully you into buying what you don't want or need.

- If you're tempted to buy something new, ask yourself if you don't already own that thing. Sounds silly, but you'd be surprised how many people buy the same thing over and over again.

- Ask yourself honestly what role your emotions are playing in the decision to buy. Act rationally, not out of fear or boredom.

- Ask yourself if there is something else you can buy for the same amount of money that would make you happier. This can be a surprisingly good method of snapping your attention back to your priorities.

Day 11

A Budget That Feeds You

Many people start whittling down expenses in the food area first and for good reason. Food costs are incredibly easy to control and with just a bit of foresight and planning, you can spend much, much less money on food and scarcely notice it. The key to successful shopping is to prepare well. Budgeting starts way before you even leave your home to go to the store.

First, lists are your friend. You can play around to see what works for you, but whatever you do, don't walk into a store with only a vague idea of what you're after. Do this and the shop may convince you that what you're after is a dozen fancy donuts and some champagne.

Some people have success choosing a few weekly recipes they like and then buying the appropriate ingredients, others choose very basic foods like cuts of meat, salad ingredients and simple vegetables so they can make straightforward things on a whim. Still more people plan what they'll eat for the week depending on what's in season or on special. Different approaches will work for different diets and lifestyles.

Whatever you decide to go for, here are a few tips that will shave money off your final bill - and, more importantly, won't make you feel like you're depriving yourself:

- Get fresh fruits and vegetables at a farmers' market. Find things that haven't been cut / prepared in any way and without packaging - they're usually the cheapest and freshest.

- When it comes to household non-perishables (salt, toilet paper, things like rice and beans, spices) buy in bulk and buy no-name brands - what's inside the box is usually identical to smaller, branded items, only cheaper.

- Make use of coupons and discounts. Loyalty cards are also a great idea and the savings really do add up.

- Join up with a friend to buy in even bigger bulk at bulk stores - split a monthly purchase and you save a lot, plus make friends with other thrifty people.

- Invest in a slow cooker or pressure cooker, buy more affordable cuts of meat and make delicious stews that are hearty and cheap.

- Rely more on non-animal sources of protein: eating beans, tofu or eggs instead of meat can be an interesting way to mix things up.

- Fast. Seriously. You don't need to eat constantly. Skip a meal or two when you've overindulged and give your system a break. Your waistline and your bank balance will breathe a sigh of relief.

Day 12

Find Your Inspiration

A lot of the time, trying to make meaningful changes to your life can feel like lonely work. Especially if you're trying to spend less money or spend it more mindfully, you might discover that you're embedded in a world where friends, family and everyone in between is encouraging you to do otherwise.

What to do? We're all social creatures, and laboring away at a mission all alone is difficult. So, don't do it alone! Find people who are on the same mission as you, and you instantly get the validation and support of those who "get" what you're doing.

You may be able to sniff out people on social media that can inspire you as you go about your life, or start following blogs of people who have similar incomes, similar lifestyles and similar goals as you. Even reading a story of someone who has dug themselves out of debt can do something powerful: *convince you that what you're doing is possible.*

Today's exercise: find a source of inspiration and support for your new mission. Read a biography of an inspirational person you admire, create a vision board of quotes or pictures that motivate you, or join a group - real or online - where people share their mission to live more frugal, more meaningful lives.

A quick note about what I'll call here "demotivation": let's say you've decided you're just not interested in spending as much as you do on weekend drinks anymore. Your friends say they understand, but they take subtle digs at you being "cheap" and antisocial, and gradually stop inviting you out, or turn down your invitations to do more affordable activities.

Whether you're trying to lose weight, save money or build your career, you might encounter people along the way who do not have your best interests at heart, and who are threatened and unhappy about you improving or changing. This is a bit of a sad thought, but if this is a problem for you, you'll need to figure out a way to manage this sort of negativity in your life.

If you have friends or family members who are more interested in you staying the same for their sake than they are in you being happier and more fulfilled, you may find yourself in the awkward position of having to rethink your connection to them. Spend some time thinking about what you'll do if you encounter resistance from others and how you'll affirm your new goals.

Day 13

Zooming Out

It's all about the money.

But in a lot of ways, it has nothing to do with money at all. Today's exercise is to take a moment to pause and have a look at where you are in your process and how your new budget is panning out. If you have a journal, whip it out and put down some of your thoughts and ideas.

Today, let's look past the money and see what's behind it.

1. What is your relationship to money? If money was a person, what would your relationship be like? Is money like an elusive lover, a punishing mother figure or a friend who helps you get stuff done?

2. How much does money play a part in your identity as a human being?

3. Think back to something you bought that you unequivocally felt made your life better. What was it? Why was this thing so special?

4. Think back to something you bought and later regretted buying. What happened?

5. Do you really want to be doing this challenge, or are you doing it because you should, or because you have to?

6. If money was no longer an issue, what would you do with your life?

How can you start doing those things now, with what you do have?

7. Take a look at yourself right now in this moment. What item on/near you is the single most important? What things could you do without?

8. Think of something you want and then decide not to buy it. How do you feel? Is it really so bad to stay in desire and want, not rushing to fill every need that pops up?

9. How do you feel about charity - both giving and receiving it? Does charity's place in your budget reflect your values?

Day 14

Zooming in Again

Ok, let's get back to the nitty gritty. Answer me this; you have two choices. One choice is to have 3 million dollars handed to you right now, in this moment, and the other choice is to have a single penny. The trick is that the single penny will double in value every day for 31 days.

Which do you choose?

Though the penny might not seem like much then and there (even after a week or two it still wouldn't seem as much as 3 million dollars) it eventually compounds and adds up to much, much more after 31 days.

A good budget doesn't have to do miracles or save you huge amounts of money all at once. In fact, it's these small steps and little amounts that sometimes build up the most - if you give them enough time.

Small expenses add up, but so do small savings.

Here are some ways to save small bits of money here and there. The great thing about small savings is that they're easy to do and you don't really notice them, but over time they build and grow.

- Carpool or consider cheaper commuting options like cycling, a scooter or even working from home.

- Go on cheaper but equally fun holidays: camping, volunteering at festivals, nature walks, couchsurfing or home swapping where you only pay the airline fee, volunteering on an organic farm to discover the countryside,..

- Ramp up your cooking skills until you can create meals on par with those in fancy restaurants - it's not that difficult with practice, you'll save money and you'll develop a valuable and fun skill too.

- Look at barter sites or Craigslist to find free items or items to trade. It may take a bit more time, but you'd be surprised at the bargains you find!

- Create a clothing swap group with your friends - get rid of clothing that's great but doesn't fit you or match your style, and get in return clothes that do.

- In this same vein, join makeup or clothing swap subreddits and you can even exchange unwanted goodies with people from all over the world. A great way to socialize.

- Quit the gym and combine a hobby with physical exercise. A dance class, hiking, climbing or sports can double as fun and exercise.

- With discipline, you can get a good workout at home for free using weights, a Pilates ball and a mat. Focus on bodyweight exercises. Get a few exercise DVDs or watch a short workout video on YouTube for ideas. When all else fails, splash out on a good pair of shoes and go jogging.

- Go digital. E-books are cheaper and save space.

- Switch off lights, devices and heaters/geysers when they're not in use. It takes you a second of thought and can save a lot in the long term.

Thrifty vs. minimalist vs. cheap

Everyone knows an insufferable scrooge. The kind of person who'll steal toilet paper from a gas station or use a tea bag 3 times just to save money. Of course, everyone has their own threshold for what counts as being smart with money and what counts as ...well, being cheap.

A lot of budgeting and thrifty living advice out there is all about the bottom line: what's the least you could do? What's the cheapest thing? It's a question of how low you can go and if you want to really save, then you can go ahead with homemade toothpaste, candles and second hand underwear.

The trouble is that living this way sucks, plain and simple. What does it matter if you shave a few cents off your lunch bill if you're utterly miserable doing it? There's a difference between being a minimalist and being miserly. A minimalist enjoys life. The goal is not to do with less, the goal is to find those things you truly need and forget the rest.

If you've ever read any advice on how to be thrifty, you may have noticed a creeping sense of sadness. And of course you would - being cheap and restrictive sends a sneaky message to your subconscious: you are not worth it, you need to take up less space, resources are scarce and you need to suffer.

How could you be happy and joyful and creative in such a state?

In other words, if you save 5 cents by getting a product so cheap and nasty it makes you feel bad about yourself and life in general, you've made a bad deal indeed. Rather spend the extra 5 cents and pay the premium for peace of mind.

Today's goal is to see where you can cut down on expense but with one caveat: you will not sacrifice safety, peace of mind or self-esteem while you do so.

Day 15

Review Your Failures

So? How are you doing?

Come on, confess. If you've "failed", don't worry. Today, you're going to look at all the ways you've failed to meet your goals. Instead of feeling bad about it though, you're going to use this as valuable information. Small failures are clues. They let you know where your idea of your ideal life and your actual life are not matching up. Didn't save as much as you wanted? Blew a bit of money on an unnecessary purchase? Back to the drawing board with you.

Today's task: find out where your new budget isn't working ...and make it work. Adjust your goals or your attitude, then check in again later.

Day 16

Celebrating and Integrating

On the other hand, if you find yourself making any little successes, you're going to do the opposite: you're going to blow them right out of proportion. You're going to praise yourself and adjust your self-identity: you're the kind of person who makes good money decisions.

Kill self-talk that sounds like this:

"Oh I'm so bad with money"
"A holiday in the Bahamas? Sounds nice but I could never afford something like that"
"I'm not good at math and all that finance stuff"
"I'll be paying off loans until I'm 100 years old"
"What can I say, I'm a bit of spendthrift!"

Don't talk yourself out of success. If you've reached a goal, no matter how small, stop and enjoy your achievement. Remember it. These are the first few steps of your new life, your new identity and your new lifestyle. So celebrate (responsibly, of course!).

Day 17

Shake Things up With a Challenge

K eep going!

A money challenge can be a fun way to mix things up, to keep you engaged and challenge some assumptions you may still be holding onto. And they're fun.

Here are some interesting challenges to flex those newly developing financial skills:

1. Challenge yourself to have a "buy nothing" day. Or week, if you're feeling brave.

2. Start a "6 item challenge" where you vow to only wear 6 items of clothing in a month - flex those creative muscles and have fun with accessories.

3. Decide to only get your groceries from a market for a month, or challenge yourself to cook meals at home every day for two weeks.

4. Give yourself a week or a day where you challenge yourself to spend half or a third of what you usually do. It can actually be quite fun to find creative ways to eat, put together an outfit or plan a trip.

5. Challenge yourself to make dinner tonight with only what you already have in the fridge, or go to that event without buying a new outfit, or

do a household chore without buying new tools or items - get creative! You can have a lot of fun repurposing, "upcycling" or plain old making do with what you already have.

6. Host a yard sale and use the money to buy something you've wanted for a long time, a holiday or a special experience that doesn't rely on material things to be enjoyable.

7. Go out and volunteer and experience how meaningful activities can be without focusing on money.

8. Instead of spending money on movies, concerts or other expensive events, get curious about communities and Meetup groups in your area that are free and give you the chance to explore your city ...and the people that live there.

9. Entertain without breaking the bank - have a potluck evening or host a night based around an activity, like board or card games.

Day 18

Experiences vs. Things

You may already have experience with the idea that a holiday is more a state of mind than anything else. Have you ever gone on a big, expensive and complicated vacation only to feel stressed the whole time and come back home to what is really relaxing - sitting on the couch in your pajamas and doing nothing?

I'm sure you can also remember a time where you had good food, good company and an atmosphere that was so enjoyable you still remember it now. Chances are, this event wasn't particularly expensive.

Holidays really are all about the experience.

In a lot of ways, stressing about the expenses can actually make a holiday less enjoyable. You've saved for months, the pressure is on to have a good time, but everything is regimented and pricey - exactly the conditions under which you'll feel stressed and obligated. So, this year, try to go on holidays that emphasize the experience and de-emphasize all the stressful and costly things that go with it.

Go to countries or areas that are less popular or less developed. Or, choose a destination that's just around the corner - you'd be surprised at how many amazing places are just under your nose. Go to places where you have friends you could stay with, or start learning about house swapping or couch surfing - it's not just for broke students.

Rent a bicycle to make a fun experience of getting around instead of the hassle of a rented car that needs to be parked and filled with gas. If you're adventurous, hitch hike. Book tickets at the last minute to save some money, and carpool when you arrive. Go on a campervan trip or stay in budget hotels and focus instead on (cheap) activities like hiking, exploring new cities on foot or enjoying public monuments and museums, which are usually quite affordable.

When you're out of the expensive resorts and break away from planned tours and the like, you get to see all the (cheap) awesome places the locals eat, or get to try your hand cooking at home with interesting new ingredients. Another option is to work in exchange for lodging - small farms often have programs like this, or you could au pair for a short time and get days off in the week to explore another country.

Today's task: think of a place you'd like to visit and get curious about the ways you could holiday there. If it seems a little out of reach right away, start putting some room in your budget to save for an end of year vacation.

Day 19

Love What You Do, Do What You Love

The common understanding is that work is on one side of the equation, and happiness is on the other. You only work so that you can afford to buy the things that make you happy. Trouble is, this is a pretty limited way of thinking about the world, yourself, and what you have to offer.

Maybe you know a person who has managed to monetize their hobbies, or eventually started to do the things they loved as their main occupation. This kills two birds with one stone: you get to have fun and do what you love, and at the same time you spin a bit of extra money. Use this money to feed back into your hobby, to indulge in a nice dinner once in a while, to pay down credit card debt or to save for gifts for that special holiday.

A side hobby can be a lot of fun, and a nice way to learn business skills, socialize and indulge in what you really care about. If you love fashion and clothing, you could sell your services as a personal shopper, or sew novelty items and sell them at monthly markets and fairs. If you love cooking, what about occasionally making a batch of cupcakes to sell at the office?

Many people generate a nice side income selling art and crafts on sites like Etsy, or join an amateur drama or comedy club that brings in money for them and their communities. Coach a sport, offer to give massages, host or organize parties, cater for events, rent out a spare room, write a recipe book, do makeup for brides or learn to do manicures, offer dog walking services or foster puppy guide dogs, babysit, become a tour guide... the list really is endless.

Today's task: brainstorm a few fun ways to let your hobbies and interest generate a bit of cash. Remember, the primary goal is to have fun, so don't get bogged down into making lots of money at first. Although, honestly, if you love what you do and are good at it, that is always a possibility...

Day 20

Stock Take and Taking a Break

We are nearing the end of this 21 day budget challenge. If you have been journaling, now is the time to go right back to the beginning and have a look at your initial goals. Take a moment to appreciate what has changed, and what you are still in the process of changing. Be kind to yourself with those goals that take a little longer, and celebrate all those good new habits you've put in place.

Today's task: take it easy and have a look at how you've fared over these past few weeks. Choose something to splash out on that will help you celebrate sticking to this challenge and having the determination to learn new and better habits. Maybe you buy a symbolic gift for yourself in the form of a nice new wallet or a cute piggy bank. Maybe you have a celebratory meal or take a weekend trip somewhere nice to unwind.

Day 21

...and Beyond

Here are some fun resources you may get inspiration from as you feel out all the corners of your new minimalist, thrifty and more meaningful life:

https://www.couchsurfing.com is a great place to start snooping around for fun new holiday ideas ... just stay safe out there!

https://www.luxuryhousesit.com, https://www.mindmyhouse.com and https://www.trustedhousesitters.com are great places to set up a profile and start applying for amazing house sitting jobs all over the world.

Check out Craigslist in your area for ads of all kinds or do a quick Google search for any barter websites in your country to swap and trade valuable items.

http://instructables.com is a paradise for DIYers, upcyclers and those who want new and fun ways to work magic with what they already have.

Look up the 21-Day Minimalist challenge on Amazon if you want to learn more about this lifestyle.

http://www.theminimalists.com is a wonderful blog with interesting reads and podcasts about minimalism and leading a more meaningful life.

http://www.missminimalist.com is a fun blog for fashion conscious but also money conscious people - read about ways to preserve and care for clothing, how to do a capsule wardrobe challenge or where to get beautiful, affordable clothing.

how to do a capsule wardrobe challenge or where to get beautiful, affordable clothing.

Conclusion

Like all good things in life, meaningful change happens slowly and gradually. You won't throw out your old life and get a magical new one in just 21 days (sorry!) but you will certainly start to unravel old and unhelpful habits, question underlying assumptions about money and wealth, and start making realistic moves towards a life that actually means something to you.

Anybody can save money. Anybody can be thrifty or even stingy. But it takes time and effort to be that person who spends money wisely. I hope that at the end of this challenge, you are one step closer to becoming that person!

Other 21-Day Challenges you may enjoy!